Memorializing

Tayleigh Folden

Presentation by *BookLeaf Publishing*

Web: www.bookleafpub.com

E-mail: info@bookleafpub.com

ISBN: 9789357745789

First edition 2023

DEDICATION

To my family, without whom these
memories never would have happened.

ACKNOWLEDGEMENT

I would like to thank Professor Robert King, who helped me rediscover poetry.

A Light Show in Ohio

It's an odd time of year for fireworks - the end of November. It's to bring in the holiday season, to make sure St. Nick can see our Ohio city from way up in the North Pole. The weather stings my nose and curls my toes - searching for warmth that doesn't exist.
That doesn't matter - not when the fireworks captivate my attention like I've never seen them before.
The first firework sounds, a loud resounding BOOM that nestles itself in my chest, like the excitement itself has popped. The crowd ooohs and aaahs with each red and gold spark that blazes across the sky. I wonder where they go once they die.
The middle part of the show is where the explosions lose their novelty. We've seen just about every variation of ways fireworks dance in the air - the music is what maintains interest. Children squirm, people check their phones, I wonder which song will be next.
But then,
The Finale comes on all at once.
What were once red, green and white shimmers in the sky transform into a gold and copper mirage of sparks. They come one right after the

other, lighting up the sky so bright you could close your eyes and believe the sun had risen.

The cacophony of sound rattles my skeleton in its place, every BOOM resonating somewhere deep- somewhere I can't reach.

The final firework rockets into the sky- a glittering copper trail gives away its trajectory. It pops with one last resound BOOM- slotting everything back into place.

Gold sparks rain down over the sky,

Shimmering,

Shimmering,

Shimmering,

Before becoming one with the stars.

The crowd roars, the music swells- but I'm stuck with the stars.

The booming, shimmering stars.

Summer

The sun filtering through the trees provides a harsh heat, a perfect juxtaposition to the cool water. Our fingers pruned long ago, but they haven't called out that The food's ready, so we don't even know we're hungry. We're too caught up in war and potions and who has the best dive to worry about such trivial things. Later we'll catch fireflies and frogs and weave our way through adults who've had one too many. But now the food is ready, and we're starving.

Celebration of Life

Despite the reason we're all here, it's joyful. A room full of people I love most, all laughing and drinking and remembering. Grandma is making her rounds, everyone seems to want her attention. I already talked with her tonight, briefly, as there seemed to be 15 hands pulling her away. My father and uncles are also making rounds filled with hugs and beer and belly laughs. I got my turn with them as well, conversed with them and laughed away the tears. My great-aunts, just as important as my grandmother, have been hugged and spoken too accordingly. The only cousin vaguely my age had left early for a school dance, and the older cousins were gathered together near the bar. I'll have to find someone else to bother. My eyes flick across the crowd, searching for my grandpa's familiar frame-
Oh.
Right…

Where Did They Go?

Raindrops putter into the water surrounding me.
I'm small, and transfixed
by the ripples created from each drop.
The ripple casts itself out,
spreading out as far as it can,
before inevitably colliding with its siblings.
The water waves its goodbye,
stilling for a mere moment
before the next drop falls.
My mother is calling for me,
but when I turn to call back,
She is gone.

I Knew

Something's wrong.
My heart is beating
two paces left
of where it should be.

Something's wrong.
There's a disturbance
in my universe,
some point I can't place.

Something's wrong.
I sit on the bed,
staring at my phone,
at the picture of her last moments.

I knew Something Was Wrong

State Champion

I can't even hear the crowd.
I'm breathless and laughing
and suddenly there's too much
in my body, so I just shake it out.
I'm not crying like I thought I would,
but that's not really me, is it?
I think I hear my mom and my friends
cheering me on in front of the stage.
But there's more than them,
there's a whole auditorium.
And all I can do is
Laugh, laugh, laugh.

Are You Out of Town?

No, why?
Your grandpa's in the hospital.
Oh.
He's ok for now.

I wish it was now

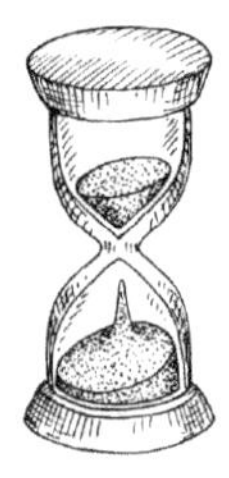

Cousins Club

We're posted up in the green room, named such due to the grass-like concrete carpet that covers the floor. We chose this room because that's where the food is, and it's not in the over-warm, crowded house. The buzzing space heater is doing its best to warm our little haven, but the winter wind creeps its way through the large windows. We don't mind. We only care about "spying" on the adults and our never-ending supply of cherry tomatoes and chocolate chip cookies. Adults come in and out in a steady stream to steal our food and ask about school. We shrug out noncommittal answers, who can think of school at a time like this? We're the rulers of our kingdom at the long-awaited family Christmas Eve party, and someone said Santa has just arrived.

Grandpa Used to Smoke

It's that time of night.
Cigarette smoke coils into unreadable cursive in
the air, the smell stings my nose. The smoke
intertwines with a raspy, country melody and the
voice of my uncle. He croons for the wish of
more time, the regret of time lost. Watch
carefully and it's as if the cursive smoke curls
into lyrics, takes the invisible notes and brings
them to my father's ear. My dad, one of the
strongest people I know, eyes far off and glassy,
listening. Our loss is fresh, fresh enough that the
burn in our eyes can't be attributed to the
cigarette he's smoking. I stare into the tabletop
fire, watch as the cigarette smoke curves up and
around the flames, a dance - the fire leads. The
smoke twirls up, turning wispy, ghostly, before
fading away into a peaceful sleep. I wish to
follow the smoke - maybe it can take me to see
him - but I lay here with these reminders instead.
 A father, a melody, and the smoke.

First Ride

The Beast roars as we fly across the hill,
whipping past sprawling fields and miniature
dirt roads.
I loosen my grip, glance sideways
as Father pilots The Beast onwards,
to see the rippling land and unblemished sky.
He never slows, but as time lags,
the wind is creating waves in the sea of grass.
As we careen onward,
Father will find a hill to conquer,
but it's as if my helmet forgot my head.
It left it on the seagrass and burning dirt road.

Bi, Bi, Bi

I don't have a ceiling fan,
otherwise I'd be watching it
go round and round and round.
I had always been odd,
but months and months and months
of deliberating had led me here,
Realizing just how odd I am.
Well, shit.

Cookie Day

I've been put in charge of chocolate chip cookies, per usual. The younger kids are put to icing sugar cookies and Mom is trying a new recipe, again. Grandma is undeterred in her mission to be everywhere all at once, and my aunt is laughing at her while she makes her turtle cookies. After I finish this batch, I'll move on to my personal favorite: buffalo chips. They're a family recipe, simple to make and the most delicious to eat. We don't need anymore cookies, the no bakes and sugar cookies and snickerdoodles and peanut butter cookies and oreo balls and oatmeal raisin cookies and peanut butter blossoms and white macadamia nut cookies and even more I forgot we made are proof of that. But buffalo chips are my cookies, coming all the way from my paternal side of my family to this side. Thankfully they don't mind, we're always more than willing to share.

It's So You

Mom pointed it out.
It seems I was too busy
crying to notice.
It wasn't your red flannel,
or the pack of Marlboros in the front pocket.
It wasn't your slicked-back hair
or closed cerulean eyes.
I turned to the one you loved,
the one you left behind,
and cried, cried, cried,
Because even Death
couldn't wipe the smile off your face.

The Music Saw Inside

The bass thrums in my veins
and the drums beat to my heart.
My hair is dyed blue, green, red
as the lights whirl in the air.
I'm far too close to the speakers,
I can already hear the high-pitched ringing
that will haunt me when the night's over.
It's worth it, though,
when the music reaches inside me
and takes my ghost in its hand.

I was in the Woods when They got the News

I was just checking the trail again,
making sure our markers were clear
so our victims wouldn't get too lost.
I found a large tree off the path,
the perfect place for contemplation.
As I stood on the tree,
I listened to the chatter of the house,
the sound of the monsters
that would later haunt the woods.
We all knew our places,
the food was laid out,
and the chairs sat around the fire.
This would be our best haunted trail yet,
even the crickets seemed to agree.
They chirped their assurances
as I meandered out of the woods.
Why was the house so quiet?

Dare Not Disturb

The blanket across my legs is soft and a tad too warm, much like the heavy weight settled across my chest. The Void purrs, nestling further into my neck, its cold nose pressing under my jaw. Such a position makes reading a hassle, but I dare not to move. Disturbing the Void is to risk its fierce copper eyes piercing your skull. Thankfully it's cozy, and I wouldn't want to be anywhere else.

He Built Me a Scooter?

Did you build it for me?
Did you build it for my cousin?
It was for one of us,
your only two grandchildren.
I don't remember the details.
Only that there was a scooter
and that you were there.

I Should Remember

I'm fragmented
The events and details of my life
slip through the cracks in my cranium
So maybe I've lied to you
Maybe these are just echoes of a past
that might not have happened
I wouldn't know